OUR HAPPINESS   OUR TEARS

IT CAN Happen

OUR "SURVIVED IT ALL TOGETHER" STORY

BY **DARRYL & MONICA**

IT CAN HAPPEN

Copyright ©2018 Darryl & Monica Sampson

Relationships, Dating, Marriage, Self-Improvement, Self-Awareness

All rights reserved. No part of this book may be reproduced, distributed, or transmitted in any form or by any means; including electronic or mechanical. This includes the use of graphics, photocopy, recording, taping or by any informative storage or retrieval system, without the written permission of the publisher. This excludes reprints in the context of reviews, testimonials, quotes or references, and certain other noncommercial uses permitted by copyright law.

PUBLISHING
Empowering The World, One Book At A Time

SHERO Publishing
3012 Quillin Court, Raleigh, NC
SHEROPublishing.com
Contact the Publisher: EricaPerryGreen@gmail.com

Cover Photography & Captions- NicoCar Productions- La, California
Cover Design: Vila Design
Book Graphics: Greenlight Creations - glightcreations.com
Printed by: Impress Print & Graphics ~ P.O. Box 13794 RTP, NC 27709

Printed in the United States of America

Disclaimer: This publication is sold with the understanding that the authors are not engaged in rendering psychological or medical services. If assistance is needed, the services of a competent professional should be sought.

Library of Congress Cataloging-in-Publication Data
ISBN-10: 0-9994470-6-8
ISBN-13: 978-0-9994470-6-2

For additional copies or booking engagements contact:
www.darrylmonica.com or darrylmonica99@gmail.com

Acknowledgements

First, we'd like to give honor and thanks to God for allowing our marriage to be the poster child for this book. We are forever grateful to Him for manifesting such great wisdom, experience and overcoming power through our willingness to hold fast to the blueprint of our marriage. We give thanks and love to our children, who never judged us while we were being groomed into the vessels we are today. They hung in there with us, saw our tears, heard our disappointments and yet loved us the same. Our children are the reason why we push so hard to encounter the life we know we were made to live. To all the Pastors, Bishops, Clergy, mentors, family and friends who have encouraged us down the years, prayed for us, blessed us and genuinely wanted the best for us. We say thank you and we love you dearly.

To my Love (**Darryl**)**,** Babe you know how I feel about you and anyone who truly knows me knows how I feel about you. Words alone can't express my passion, compassion and my adoration I feel for you. You have made my life extremely enjoyable even when there seemed to be no

IT CAN HAPPEN — DARRYL & MONICA

joy I could find. We are now embarking on the best years of our lives and I boldly say to you, let's get it Babe. VISION is what we are all about. - *Monica*

To my Promise (**Monica**), I always tease you about taking me from the crib, but God allowed what was destined for now to be established back then. Even to this day many are baffled and yet confused as to how and why, failing to realize it was simply because of Him! Thank you for allowing me to be the man the Father has created for you. I love you with an everlasting love. As we continue to mature in our union of love, I can't help but to be excited about the intensity of waking up to you, kissing you, yeah…touching you, and most of all, dreaming with you. Who said fairytales don't come true. Love you girl! - *Darryl*

The Authors

Meet Darryl

Darryl Sampson, the former Houstonian, now resides in Burbank, California. He is a leader, compassionate about the will of God & His people. Darryl has served as founding senior Pastor, Youth Pastor & is the CEO of L.Y.R.R.A.D. (Living Young, Righteous, Radical, And Dedicated) Inc.

Darryl is a visionary, musician, mentor, entrepreneur & dynamic speaker. He has shared in churches, conferences, workshops, & seminars; stressing the importance of living a Godly lifestyle through holiness and spiritual growth. With a God-given drive & strong passion for youth, Darryl has a way of setting the atmosphere and stirring the audience to seek the Lord and to know Him intimately.

Darryl is one of the up and coming anointed voices in the Body of Christ. With dynamic delivery, Darryl operates in the prophetic and healing and is a highly prolific preacher and teacher. Darryl's current projects include debut books, conferences, seminars, gospel concerts and business endeavors. Darryl Sampson or Pastor D is a sought out individual in the Body of Christ.

Meet Monica

While Monica Sampson currently resides in Burbank, CA, she is originally from Houston, Texas. Monica serves as an Intercessor, worshiper, author, entrepreneur and exercise extremist. She is a proud graduate of Booker T. Washington High School (Houston, Texas). Monica serves alongside her husband, Darryl, in several ministries including there own. With the help of God, Monica has worked towards bringing deliverance to people in bondage. It is Monica's determination and no-nonsense attitude that have led her to affectionately adapt a heart for marriages that have come under attack. Monica is a woman who is extremely dedicated to seeing marriages restored, revived and renewed.

Introduction

To all our readers, we want you to know that we are not writing our story to transform anyone's life because only God possesses that kind of power for those who have a made-up mind. You can read all the best top selling books on how to become a better you, have a wonderful marriage or a great career, but if you don't change the pattern of your thoughts, you will NEVER reach your God-given destiny. We are one of the many couples who decided to change our thought behaviors and once we did, change began to affect every area of our lives.

This is a true story of how a marriage not only survived but has conquered all the fiery darts thrown by the enemy, which involves sexual and emotional infidelity, external family battles, internal fears, depression fueled by low self-esteem, financial and emotional struggles, etc.

We are compelled to speak into, encourage, inform and strengthen marriages. We're not afraid or embarrassed to share our story nor our truths. When I was young and did something very awful people would say, "You should be ashamed of yourself." Well we beg to differ in this instance because the awful things that are a part of our journey helped us discover who we really are and the purpose of our being. The scripture says, *"Therefore, there is no condemnation for those who are in Christ Jesus, because through Christ Jesus the law of the Spirit who gives life has set you free from the law of sin and death"* (**Romans 8:1-3, NIV**). Our trials in life have helped pave the pathway to triumph. If our testimony can help breathe an ounce of life into a lifeless marriage or individual, then we will gladly tell it every chance we get. We speak a blessing over every union and individual reading this book. *-Darryl & Monica-*

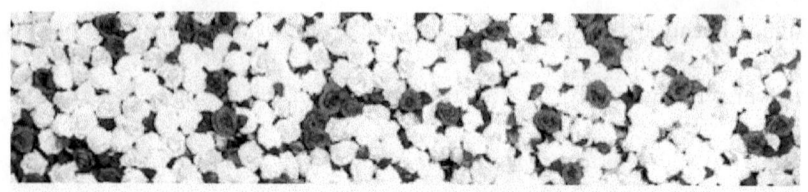

Table of Contents

-HER STORY-

The Fight	13
The Great Wakeup	23
The Emotional Entanglement	42

-HIS STORY-

The Fight	63
The Great Wakeup	70
The Emotional Entanglement	80

THEIR STORY

It Can Happen (Monica)	85
It Can Happen (Darryl)	90

No relationship is all sunshine, but two people can share one umbrella and survive the storm together.

Her Story

A memoir of a woman who encountered her own battles within herself, family and marriage, to discover it was all a part of her making into the vessel she is today. I now know who I am and the fabric I am made of. Who am I?
I am a woman of great worth, love, compassion, perseverance and full of victory.

THE FIGHT

Getting in the trenches to do battle with the true enemy that threatens your right to claim stake or to permanently lay hold of the promises of God.

Matthew 11:12 *says, "The Kingdom of heaven suffereth violence and the violent take it by force."*

The year was 1999 when my life changed forever. I had my first child and was happily wed on August 21st. There we were young, broke and in love. We had no plans for the future. Our minds were not on a savings account, going to college or even what we'd hoped to accomplish in the next 5 years. We were so in the moment of living. Our wedding literally cost us about $100.00 and some change and for our honeymoon, our uncle paid for a hotel room for the night. That was it, nothing glamorous or spectacular, but you couldn't tell us the whole ordeal wasn't. We said our vows and started life as husband and wife, Mr. and Mrs. Darryl L. Sampson. Neither one of us knew what we were signing up for; we didn't know how to take care of our own selves, let alone each other. We had no clue on how to successfully be married, but we were willing to give it our all. I had no real example of what a true marriage looked like.

My mother had always been the dominate person in her relationships and always seemed to date a "yes" man. You know the type of men that said yes to everything when she put her foot down. I had no clue on what it meant to be a submissive wife. I never had my father in my life so there was an unrecognized brokenness there I had never dealt with. I was a young woman who dealt with severe depression, low self-esteem and had come into this marriage with undiscovered dormant issues that would play out in the years to come. At the time, all we were concerned about was doing it right before God.

Growing up in church, we constantly heard the word "shacking", which was a word used to describe a woman & man living under the same roof without being married. Oh how we did not want the Lord to stop blessing us, so we desired holy matrimony even the more. I loved Darryl and he loved me, and as far as we could see, that's the way it was always going to be for all time. There was no other person for either one of us. He was the "Booger with the Sugar". We knew we were meant for each other, no doubt about it. And taking each other's hand before the Preacher surely meant everything else would fall right in place and would stay that way... so we thought. Having one child at the time and no jobs we really had nothing going for us but love. To me, Darryl could do no wrong and even if he did, in my eyes, some kind of way, he was still right. He was cute, well dressed and an awesome drummer; someone I'd known all my life. Growing up in the same church together gave us a firm foundation and somewhat of a friendship. Flirting and kissing each other as adolescents, sparked chemistry between the both of us at an early age. To actually find ourselves married to one another is still something people can't quite figure out to this day. The two most unlikely people found interest in one another. Me being three years older, I would have never imagined being with him for that reason alone. He housed a sensitive side and I liked it. He was gentle, calm, and inviting. Plus, he had beautiful soft hands like a girl. I loved how his breath was always fresh and rarely housed the smell of liquor. He wasn't like the norms I'd dated before. He was shorter than me and high red in complexion. Oh how I disliked short and light skinned men; two disadvantages he had from the jump. He wasn't a dog, rude or arrogant. He was meek in nature. He didn't have much but the clothes on his back and a place to lay his head, which was at his aunt's house. He had a job at the time, and although mediocre, I could see great potential in him from the beginning. The fact that he had dimples didn't hurt either. Even though he had a few things going on, still my eyes were never fixed on him until someone else noticed and made mention of him in a relational manner. This was someone who had absolutely no business looking at him in that way. Let me just say to this day I thank God for that person who had no business being interested in him, you know who you are. Her desire to be with him sparked an interest in me concerning him. What was it about him that had her so bent all out of shape? I was curious and about to see for myself.

I fell for him hard and fast. It didn't take long before he and I became a hot item. In love, in lust, whatever you want to call it, I was all for it. We were all over each other and we showed it by sexually encountering one another at every given moment. It's like we couldn't get enough. He was the first guy I had ever cried with while making love and to me he was special. Something in me knew we had created a bond like I'd never experienced before. We were always cuddling, holding hands and saying sweet words to one another. I remember not letting him off the phone late at night and he would literally fall asleep while I listened to him breathe. Yes, I was that crazy in love. Some have asked how did you know at the age of 21 that he was the one? My answer has always been there are different strokes for different folks. Everyone's experience of coming into the realization of knowing who that special person is varies and is an individual experience. I remember sitting in church and God giving me a vision showing me that he was my husband and speaking it to me in my spirit at a time I didn't even know God.

Once we went public with our relationship, we immediately had to suit up, assume the warrior's position and fight to be able to rightfully continue in our new love. At times our sanity, family bond and integrity as a union had been tampered with by others.

I remember thinking everybody can hook up and be celebrated, why not Darryl and I? When we outwardly declared our interest in one another we encountered stares, looks and whispers etc. We literally had more against us than those who were for us. It was so bad you could literally count on one hand how many people celebrated our relationship. I remember going to the church we attended at the time and feeling the tension as we walked in for services. Something was different; something was odd.

When we were interested in other people everything was cool, people talked to us, smiled at us, but once the news hit concerning our courtship, all of a sudden, we were an outcast amongst people we'd known all of our lives, or at least a great deal of it.

We were so young and at times we would hurt behind the lack of support for this fresh new love we were experiencing. What was so wrong with Darryl and Monica being an item? Everyone could sleep with whomever they wanted to, have affairs, beat on their spouses, etc. But oh no, this idea of these two being together was absolutely out of order and a huge problem. I remember so called friends of mine turned on me, stopped dealing with me and actually began to spread gossip. How did I turn into your enemy overnight? Were we hurting anyone by being together? Were we committing some horrific crime? He was single and so was I.

One thing I'd come to realize years later is God was preparing us for something greater in the midst of all of that drama and we had no clue. Being raised in a Baptist church there was minimal talk of actually hearing the voice of God or having a strong relationship with Him. We didn't even know that existed. The most important aspects of the black church back then were the musicals being on point, having a lot of Deacons, an overly supportive Pastor's aide, active youth department, hoeing around and gossiping. We didn't know the voice of God or how He operated. We were just a couple of kids who grew up in church but had no personal relationship with God, or even knew we could.

His family had their own reserves about me and mine about him. At that time, we didn't care what anyone thought, what they had to say or what they tried to do to get us to abandon the relationship. And trust me, they tried some of the dumbest things. Things like clergymen taking Darryl out to eat just to try to convince him to end the relationship with me. I remember his mother asking me to get his clothes together and take him back to his aunt's home. I politely told her I couldn't do that, and I didn't. This was a grown man, well capable of making sound decisions. His parents even talked to his grandparents, trying to get him away from me. The more they tried, the more we pulled closer together. They were all losing a battle they could never win.

During those beginning stages of our relationship, we learned that when the world says no, you can't, you shouldn't and throw much pressure at you to try and keep you from, you need to remember if God says yes, then you can, you will and you should. *"For I know the plans I have for you declares the Lord," plans to prosper you and not harm you, plans to give you a future and a hope* (**Jeremiah 29:11, NIV**).

When people and things are trying to kill your promise, even in its infant stage, God knows how to shield you and protect the very thing He has orchestrated. My husband and I had to fight by using our spiritual weapons *(prayer, holding fast to our commitment to God and each other)*. We refused to give up on one another, even through some of the roughest times. We decided to stay together and to take care of our family to the best of our ability through all the chaos and confusion. We've been that family that got knocked down and looked over, but we always fought our way back.

There were many seasons where the fight came from family, church folk, life pressures and even our own flesh. We never questioned having to fight, but we oftentimes questioned where the battles were coming from. Encountering unnecessary stress from individuals who said they live for God should know better…so we thought. People who have the same bloodline as we do wouldn't mishandle us that way…so we hoped. Nevertheless, those same individuals tried it time after time.

One of the many lessons Darryl and I had to learn was the importance of getting past the opinions of family, which was a process in itself. We had to learn how to place all naysayers in the "THEY DON'T MATTER SECTION" of our lives. Of course, we should be mindful of the image we portray, but when people flat out judge you based on their own speculation, ignorance or hearsay, it is non-sense. The people who you think know you best really know you the least. Oftentimes people outside of your relationship have etched in their minds who you are and who you are not before they even enter a relationship with you themselves; especially miserable, lonely and broke people. Their mindset and thought capacity is already in a negative posture, which causes everything and everybody to be seen in the same regards.

Darryl and I are masters at fighting for our love now. You try to tear us apart and we will literally bite your face off (in the spirit of course lol). Through much experience, trial and error, we have come to the revelation of knowing that a love like ours first, is God ordained, rare and it is something a great number of people search their whole lives trying to find, and many don't. We guard our love with God's word, His blood and His principles.

IT'S A GUARANTEED WIN!

THE GREAT WAKE-UP

Infidelity: *a violation of a couple's assumed or stated covenant regarding emotional and/or sexual exclusivity.*

The year was 2004, five years later, married and still in love, now with 4 babies. By this time, we'd grown so spiritually in God, served on the ministerial staff together, and to our best ability, tried to follow the word of God in our everyday walk. There were times financially, when we struggled so bad, all while remaining faithful to our beliefs. Faithful to services, giving that 10% and an offering was like a ritual for us. Let's not talk about sacrificially giving. It was our middle name. Our home life I felt, was good. Our children were growing and by this time we'd just had our last two children, our beautiful twins *(Sierra & Kierra)*. Michael was 5 and Mel was 3 at the time and to me, life was going as planned. I will never forget Darryl and I sitting on the couch in the living room, as we so often did and retrieved the mail. To our surprise, a letter in the pile was addressed to him from some woman I believe from another state. In the letter it made mention something to the fact that she couldn't wait to see him. We didn't know who it was from or what it was all about, so we just discarded it like junk mail. Although I thought about it afterwards, I couldn't figure out this mystery myself, so I eventually let it go. Little did I know, the Lord was giving me a sign that I was about to encounter a trial that almost choked the very life out of me.

Me being in the position I was in caused me to totally miss the warning. When I say in the position I was in, let me expound. I thought Darryl would never hurt me. He was the perfect man of God, husband and father. My husband leaving me and messing around with another woman was impossible in our union to me. I soon found out the hard way, that God is the only one who will never leave nor forsake me for anything or anybody. Man is full of flaws and at times they will manifest. My flaw was depression and it was on display constantly in my marriage. I remember holding back sexually from him months at a time and this went on for years. The excuses of why I was not pleasing my husband were the same old lines- I'm tired, I don't feel like it or I would just totally ignore the invitation altogether. This is never an excuse for anyone to cheat, but I sure didn't give him a reason to remain faithful either. When I got married, it's like I sunk into this place of deep complacency & severe depression fast. There were times I would close myself up in a room for days, only coming out to go to work, church, eat, bath and back in my secluded space I went again. Low self-esteem sat on me hard and how I felt about myself took a toll on our relationship significantly.

Shortly after the mysterious letter incident, around Christmas time one night he called me into the living room to sit on the couch to talk. To my surprise the words that flowed from his mouth I will never forget because it punctured my heart quickly and severely. He simply says with no reserves, "I think I don't love you anymore." I'm sitting there dumbfounded thinking, "Did he just say what I think he just said?" Wait a minute, hold up, weren't we supposed to be snuggling and cuddling? I was in total shock and speechless all at the same time. It was like being instantly frozen in a moment. Immediately after he spoke those damning words, tears began to flow like a broken faucet. I was completely caught off guard and did not know how to respond. I was blindsided because I had no intuition or gut-wrenching feeling that something was wrong in our marriage. So I began to ask him questions and he simply and calmly stuck to his disclaimer. I cried so much until it looked like someone had punched me repeatedly in the face. My eyes were extremely swollen to the point I could barely see. After we finished dialoging about what he had just disclosed, he told me to go to bed and rest. The next day in shock from what he said, I still didn't understand what was really going on behind the scenes. I was naïve; things went downhill from there. All of sudden, he started leaving home to go stay at his mother's house. All while this is going on, I'm still clueless as to what was really happening. So now we're separated but he is still coming home often to see the kids. My thinking at the time was he was confused, needed space or maybe he was going through something and just needed a break. There I was working a temp assignment, all while taking care of our four children. He being a great father, never missed a beat, taking the kids with him to his mother's home on weekends. One thing about Darryl L. Sampson, he loves his children and is going to be with them no matter what.

I'm a nervous wreck not knowing what to do or how to fix this. How could I fix it when I didn't know it was broken? Where did we go wrong? This was my first marriage and first time experiencing marital conflict on this level. One day I'm chilling at home washing clothes in a good space, in spite of my marital issues and the phone rings. A very familiar but fragile voice is on the other end. This person I completely adored and knew would never lie to me. She said these very words, "I know why your husband is not at home." What did she say that for? Everything in me stood at attention. I couldn't believe what I was hearing and was eager to know the rest of what she had to say. How did she know anything about what was possibly causing my husband to leave home? She then proceeded to mention a female's name and said that basically they were together and that was the reason he was not with me. See this female who he was allegedly with was also a member at our church, so when those words rolled off my informant's tongue and into my earlobe, all I could do was hit the floor, screaming and crying for at least thirty minutes straight. I will never forget the agony and the pain I felt when I heard her say that female's name. It was like someone took my heart out of my chest, laid it on a cutting block, took a meat beater and beat it over and over. My heart bled out, the tears flowed out and the screams came out uncontrollably. Once I gathered myself off the floor, I immediately called him but my call was unanswered. There I was, an emotional mess after hearing my man was entertaining another woman. For the life of me I just couldn't think straight. It was like having a million scrambled thoughts in my mind and not being able to process any of them. This new information was too much for my mind to handle and I literally felt like I was having a panic attack. Sometime after that phone call, he came home and I asked him about the accusation and of course he denied it. There I was, blind by my love for him, not wanting to accept the fact that my man was perhaps in lust with someone else. Denial is powerful and if you fall prey to it, it will have you dismissing every trace of truth and embracing a full lie. So now he's back and forth between his parents home and ours. He gets mad, he leaves and by this time, this had become a routine. I remember his phone rang while he was in the shower and her name showed up across the screen. Why is she calling my husband I thought to myself. It must be some truth to the phone call I received from my trustworthy friend I thought. I then decided to go through his phone and that's when I saw a text message between the both of them. I could only see what she said back to him and her exact words were, "You know how to get me out of the panties." I couldn't believe it! I was hurt, but that powerful fella called denial made it seem not as bad as it really was. After he got out of the shower, I asked him why she was calling him. He replied, "Cuz' that's my friend." I asked him to tell me how she was his friend and of course he never could reply back with a legit answer. I asked him to stop talking to her and he replied again, "That's my friend." After that, I let it go because I was tired of his anger button being triggered.

Plus, I wanted him to stay home. I remember so clearly one day he got mad and decided to pack his stuff to leave. I literally fell to the ground before his feet, grabbed him by his knees, crying and begged him not to leave me. So adamant about leaving, he literally kept walking as I was being pulled on the floor, still holding on to his knees as he continued to walk and pack his clothes. Wow… I think about that now and just shake my head in disbelief. I've heard the phrase, "When you love someone, you just don't treat them bad." But this was not the case and the scene was horrific. He displayed no love for me that day. Mind you, we are still going to the same church and so was this other female. To my knowledge, this affair had been going on for about 2 to 3 months and I had no clue. One day, a meeting was called with clergy and all parties involved so that we could get to the bottom of the accusations. But him being a coward, skipped out on the meeting, which left his side female alone to speak concerning the situation. In that meeting it was basically disclosed by her that yes, they were an item and had been together sexually on several occasions. She expressed that they were in love with one another. You talk about hearing words that felt like someone had thrown me in a coffin, sealed the lid and lowered me down in the ground. That's exactly how I was left feeling. All I could do was hit the floor in total anguish. By this time, me and the floor were well acquainted. I'd never hit the floor so much in my life before. I remember that same day, right after the meeting, speaking words to the side female concerning how I felt and ultimately letting her know that I forgave her. Even to the point I literally walked over to her and hugged her as a sign of forgiveness. Wait, you mean to tell me you went and wrapped your arms around this woman and forgave her right after she told you your husband had been spending time and sleeping with her? Yes, I truly did. At that moment, it wasn't as hard as people may think. I still can't explain it. All I know is that it was nothing but a God moment and having the Holy Spirit allowed me to do this. Being the Monica that I was in the past and sometimes still could be, would have snatched her literally out of her skin and left nothing but a shell. I chose to forgive her immediately, not for her, but for me. This heart felt act of forgiveness rendered freedom to me that kept hatred from ultimately setting up in my heart and crippling my chance to be healed sooner. Understand this- when there is a greater purpose involved, the Lord has a way of rerouting our reactions. How I normally would have reacted, I couldn't. See I had been hurting so bad this whole time, that in that moment, I just wanted to be at peace and be in the Father's will for my life. I was drained and tired from all the warfare, the disappointment, the late-night cries and excruciating heartache I was experiencing. I had finally put God back as first priority in my life and it felt great. In that season I'd spent so much time with God, reading and listening to His word and meditating on Him because it kept my mind from going crazy for real. Me being totally in God's face kept me from killing someone, kept me from jail and it kept me from walking away from it all. I was so distraught, I couldn't even take care of my kids properly because grief had me so enslaved. I would try to be a mother, but I just couldn't find the strength to be what I once was to my children. To me, life felt like I was walking dead. The ordeal had left me totally numb and out of touch with reality. I couldn't eat, sleep or rationalize straight. I was a complete mess through and through. There were times I could feel a stroke coming on or at least stroke like symptoms. It was like parts of me were slowly shutting down bit by bit. My anxiety level was on high. I had to grab hold to God for dear life because His strength was the only thing keeping me alive and going. By the time the meeting occurred with clergy, pleasing God and keeping my peace was the only agenda in my heart. That's how I felt that day. Oh but my actions on the next day said something totally different.

After the meeting I went home and sat quietly. I was in a paralyzed state. Thoughts of them being together ran across my mind constantly. I called him but received no answer. So I called his parents and spoke to them, letting them know that it was true he was cheating on me. His mom's words to me literally were, "That's what you and your mother get." Her words cut like a butcher's knife, but I couldn't feel the full depth of her hurtful words because by this time I had already heard the worse of the worse. I later found out that his mom said those words to me because she still held on to unforgiveness towards my mother, who had an affair with her cousin's husband when I was a little girl. Maybe she felt this was revenge for her cousin I thought, but I really didn't care. That very night I laid out on the floor, weeping before the Lord. All of a sudden, I heard the Lord in my spirit say, "Get up and praise me." By this time there was no pride, nothing dignified left in me. I was just a weak vessel yielded to whatever God was saying and doing in my life. I just wanted to be close to God because this man was the only one holding me together. With no hesitation or questioning, I immediately leaped off the floor (butt naked) and began to dance all over that living room floor. I remember bumping into desks, the couch and end tables, but that didn't stop me. I danced like David danced, the only difference was I had no clothes on when I started dancing. I praised God like a mad woman who was desperate for deliverance. Instantly, He had turned my weeping into leaping.

I woke up the next day (Monday morning) furious, full of rage and anger. How could he do this to me? Oh you think you just gone go on with your life being with her? You think you gone get away with this? These are all the questions I pondered in my mind. I got up and rode to his parents' house and along the way I am strategizing and plotting on how I can get back at him. I get to his parents' house, park across the street out of view, I write and place a warning note on one of the cars in their driveway. The note basically was warning Darryl to watch his back, which made it seem like someone was watching their house. When I heard from him that they found the letter, I was happy glad. I literally wanted to scare the shit out of him and his family for real. Why not? He was spending time with this female over there and his family knew about it I'm thinking. I remember my son being 5 at the time, telling me that his dad had another girlfriend. How did my son know that? He knew because he was spending time with his dad over his parents' house, where she would often visit. Kids are not as naïve as we think. After I left their house I headed to the store where I purchased a sharp knife and a hammer. I quickly hopped on the freeway and headed to his job because I wasn't done yet. Revenge was all I could think of, which led me to another scare tactic. Did they think I was just going to roll over and play dead to this situation? I gave this man my life and letting go wasn't going to be that easy. Yeah, I was calm the other day but not today. If he decided to be with her, I was going to make sure they would be forever looking over their shoulders. They wouldn't know if it was me or her husband terrorizing them. I got to his job, spotted his car in the parking lot, drove in and parked. I quietly got out, looked for anyone coming, got low and headed towards his ride. As soon as I got to it, I immediately slashed all four tires, broke the side mirrors, cracked his front & back windshield and severely keyed his car. By this time an employee of the company walked out and saw me and the damage I'd done, so I immediately dashed to my car and sped away as fast as I could. Oh no, I thought to myself, what did I just do? My heart was pacing and my adrenaline was through the roof. Thoughts of going to jail bombarded my mind, but I knew deep down inside he wouldn't press charges on the mother of his kids. I made it home and called my Pastor at the time. How could I have been so anger-driven? The day before at the meeting, I was in a good place, plus my Pastor advised me to let it go. He said, "If they want to be together, let them. God will take care of it."

On the phone my Pastor calmed me down and told me to head to his house and I did. There I was comforted by his mother-in-love. She was a praying woman and boy did her presence make all the difference. I don't know how it happened. All I know is the mistress's husband ended up being there, I was there and so was Darryl. After my Pastors' mother-in-love prayed and spoke words of encouragement, I looked at my husband. I told him that I loved him and I wanted him back home. I didn't care who was around. I had tunnel vision. All I could see was he and I in the room. I declared my love for him and assured him that we could get past this, with tears streaming down my face.

He cried, told me that he loved me and he wanted to come home. He then turned to his mistress's husband, apologized to him, went and met with her, broke off the relationship and talked to our Leader about what had taken place. Can I tell you that same day my husband was back home for good because of the prayers of the righteous, the praises that were given unto God, the faith I put in Him and we been kicking it strong ever since. I was overjoyed and excited all at the same time. Finally, we felt whole again and my family was complete again. I thought everything would go back to normal… but then the hard part began *(the healing process).*

Healing had to start. I thought it would be easy, but it was the hardest part of the entire ordeal. There are things I had to factor in when I decided to forgive him, especially when dealing with something on this caliber. First of all, when you say you forgive, you better do your homework and know what that actually means because if you don't you just bought yourself a one-way ticket to a cycle of heartache, wasted time, unnecessary fights and arguments, misunderstandings, false accusations and most likely your marriage ending in divorce. Some women may say I'm crazy, but for me, part of my healing concerning his affair was I wanted to know everything that happened between him and his mistress, no matter how much it hurt me. I still say to this day I am glad I asked and that I know as much as he could provide. Another reason I'm glad I asked was it kept me from questioning things years down the road, and trust me, the mind has a way of drifting into wonderland. He told me about it and then it was over. Are there other details I may not know about? I'm pretty sure, but for the most part, I know what the root of the problem was, how it transpired and that it ended.

I was so grateful to God for bringing him home, all I wanted was to get pass this and be a better us. When you want something so bad, you are willing to do whatever it takes to get it. I wanted our marriage so to the point I constantly had to remind myself not to mention the affair when we argued. To keep emotions in check, I constantly talked to myself when I was alone because my mind would begin to reflect back on the thoughts of them together, and that would trigger the pain all over again. I had to tell myself you're not going to go through his phone, you're not going to be looking over his shoulders or start imagining you see things you really don't. At that time, I had great communication with Monica because I was always talking to myself. I was denying my flesh as much as I could of what it wanted because I knew if I didn't, instead of us moving forward, we would swap out for a merry-go-round motion instead. When you are trying to move ahead or pass something, and you start going in circles, it's a trap set to make you think you are progressing when you are really regressing. I didn't want movement, I wanted advancement, so I had to deny those insecure nudges. I had to tell myself when he was speaking to other females I knew or didn't know, that I wasn't going to micro-marriage-manage him. If I let him back in, I had to let all that other stuff out that was going to jeopardize what God was rebuilding, restructuring, restoring and reviving again.

I had to remind myself that I wasn't a private investigator. I was not going to be snooping around or hiding in bushes. I was not going to have a fit when he said he was going somewhere without me or when he was not home at the exact time he said he would be. I wasn't going to go all Rambo on him if my emotions were all over the place. Yes, I was in a vulnerable place, but God had given me the wisdom to navigate and channel that vulnerability, which allowed me to bypass all those viruses that wanted to kill the reboot, the restart and the revelation of what God was doing in our reunion. We were wiser and stronger in our walk with the Lord, which caused the same affect in our walk with one another. If the devil thought we were a force to be reckoned with before, he had no clue as to how dangerous we would be to him and his empire in the aftermath. We literally took one second at a time learning to trust, love and believe in us again. I had to reassure him that I loved and needed him more now than ever. He was dealing with so much shame and guilt until it was unreal. I had my own share too, but it was not on the level of his. He was the one who got the looks, the whispers, the nice-nasty comments and the awkward treatment. He was the one guilty of committing this sexual sin and everyone knew it. Most people showed their sympathy towards me, so I had to step it up and become his greatest cheerleader. His corner of supporters was scarce, and I did not depend on anyone else to do my job. I had to literally lay my hands on him at times and do warfare for his mind. I had to esteem him even higher behind closed doors and definitely out in public. It is my belief and one that I strongly stand by, that a spouse is the ultimate pusher when it comes to their significant other reaching their predestined place. I can only speak from a woman's point of view. I believe that we house the most powerful tool, and if used right, it will cause our men to reach their full potential in God in all areas of his life. What is that tool called? Support. It's nothing deep. Everything he will ever need to succeed is all wrapped in our support for him. Start supporting him and watch how he evolves, excels, and expands. It will be like watching a caterpillar turn into a gorgeous butterfly right before your eyes. The transformation will be life changing and beautiful to behold, because you as his number 1 supporter; as a life giver, will be able to rewind in your mind the timeline of his life and see where he was and now where he is. How I love seeing the fruit of my labor.

I chose to give him my full support. He needed it, he deserved it and he appreciated it. We must forgive even if we don't forget. They are two totally different acts. A changed mind equals changed matters. When you change your mindset, what matters to you changes. What he'd done to me, the pain I experienced, the shame and embarrassment I felt, didn't matter anymore. What mattered was us, our love, our union, our children and our legacy. I will forever remember the incident because God wants to use that as a testimony for other's journey towards healing, but I completely forgave him. The pain felt from that circumstance no longer exists, even though I know I felt it. God will bring such a healing in your life till you have to really think hard about the incident to remember all the pain caused from it, but then the love that came out of it overshadows everything negative you felt because of it. My emotions have no connection to that pain anymore. I had to let it go. It was hard at times, but again, when you want something so bad, you will do what it takes to have it. I wanted my marriage and because we chose to fight, to stand, to love, we now have a greater marriage. So again, **WE WIN**!

In the midst of this ordeal, I learned how to truly put my trust in God and completely lean on Him. There were so many valuable lessons I learned about myself and my marriage that I will never forget. I had to remember I was his permanent promise and she was simply a temporary distraction. The enemy ultimately wanted him to forfeit his promise.

Ladies, please know that the love of your heavenly Father is greater and deeper than any love you will ever experience. I learned to never put someone in the place only God belongs. I am so thankful that I was able to see my own downfalls and shortcomings and was able to repent to my husband and work on me as well. Know that God will never leave you, but your spouse can. Know that God will never stop loving you, even if your man tells you he has. Know that God will always be with you, even if your husband starts being with someone else. Who is like the Lord? NOBODY!

Special Blessing Shout-Out: *To the other lady in this experience, I speak nothing but love, joy and continued peace in your life.*

THE EMOTIONAL ENTANGLEMENT

Entanglement: *the condition of being deeply involved, the action of entangling, something that confuses or ensnares.*

The year 2013 came in just like any other year. We were trying to get back on our feet from a 9 month stay in Mississippi, where we experienced a financial crisis, coupled with a great amount of disappointment and sacrifice. Like many Christians in leadership, we felt we were called by God to relocate to Mississippi to pastor and lead a people out of traditional religious mindsets. So, in 2012, we closed down our in-home daycare business and off we went. No jobs, no money saved, just a house full of furniture and our recent tax refund of maybe 4k. I secured a place to live, enrolled the kids in school and there our lives began in Meridian. Not fully doing our research concerning the economy, we found ourselves in a bind when it came to finding stable income that would support our basic living expenses. We were not after a fancy lifestyle or costly things, we just needed funds to pay monthly reoccurring bills. At that time, we went from one dead end job to another. I went from making thousands in my home a month to making $7.15 hourly as a cashier in the grocery store. What a drastic and devastating change that was. I'll never forget seeing my first paycheck and almost crying. It was almost $300 for a 40 hour work week. Darryl landed a job as a merchandiser, stocking grocery stores with beverages and he too felt abandoned by God when he saw the net pay on his check. Yeah you guessed it, not even $300 for one week. We began to question whether or not we really heard from God. Even then, with our pockets being broke, our spirits disturbed and our minds in disbelief, we couldn't help but lean more on Him because of our current situation. We strongly believed we had great potential in ministry in this place and honestly thought we could really help produce change in the lives of the people. The struggle to survive intensified and when it was at its worse, that feeling of enough is enough arose and we made up in our minds that we could no longer live this way. By this time, Darryl's car was repossessed and mine was next, being I was about 3 months behind. He quickly made a decision to move us back to Houston, with nothing but clothes in the trunk of my Toyota

Rav 4. We loaded the rest of our things in storage and hit the highway back home.

There we were, back in Houston, trying to regain our momentum and middle-class status. I'd accepted a job as a Temp and really loved it. It was rough living with extended family, all while having my own family of six. There were challenges that really drove me to the edge and almost over the cliff. When you've had the privilege of having your own, it's difficult when you revert back to sharing living spaces. It's hard being up under someone else's roof, rules and regulations, when you yourself have your own. The living arrangement only worked for a short period of time and we knew we had to make other plans quickly and we did. We eventually moved into our own two-bedroom apartment. The year 2013 looked promising as we began to rebuild our lives and regain substance. Life was looking good and I was optimistic and overjoyed that we had our own place again. We had the freedom to move freely when we wanted and how we wanted. There's truly nothing like it. We were back serving in ministry and all was going right in our lives. Then out of nowhere, I entered a season of temptation unlike I had ever experienced before.

He had been watching me at work perform my job duties day after day to my surprise. He approached me and asked me a simple question, as if he was trying to get me to notice him on purpose. He asked, "Do you want my email?" I looked up at him and replied, "No, I don't need it." It wasn't what he said that stuck out to me, but the way he said it set off an alarm in my mind. See the position at my job at that time involved me helping out the guys in the warehouses, whether it was providing documents via email or giving them work items needed to perform their job duties. He needed something only I could provide. As time went on, we casually spoke to one another. Nothing major, but I could tell he was digging me or at least I thought he was. At the same time, I wasn't tripping because he was sweet on the eyes and seemed like a gentlemen. What was it about him that caught my attention? I'd seen plenty of good looking, nice men, but never did they catch my undivided attention. Was it the fact he was of another race, maybe his soft bad boy image? Was it his smile, blue eyes, his sensitivity or that he loved God, so he portrayed? It could have been all of the above. I remember us having a conversation about how our spouses had cheated on us. There it was. Something relatable we could converse about that blew the adultery door wide open and gave possibility an opportunity. There I was playing the victim role when supposedly I was a victor. If I was an overcomer, why was I talking about this with him? It was none of my business what he'd gone through. There was no point, no reason in sharing this information and it definitely was not for testimony purposes. It was that quick. We both let the enemy play us and from there, the wrong conversations became frequent.

Never in a million years did I think my attention would be fixated on another man the way it was for him. At one point he embodied my whole thought pattern. Was I feeling vulnerable and didn't recognize it? How could this happen to someone like me? I was a person focused on God and my family. Was it something I said or did? Was it something that was missing in my life that allowed this door to present itself? Was I really seeking more than what I had at home and just didn't know it? Was it payback for what Darryl had done to me previously? I would often ponder these questions but could never reach a solid answer.

First of all, how could I let myself feel this strong attraction for another man period, not to mention a married man? Things emotionally progressed extremely fast. Before I knew it, we were saying things to one another that people who have spouses shouldn't say to another person outside of the marriage. We would meet in certain places at work just to exchange a couple of words. Things like how we wanted to see each other outside the workplace. Although our conversations were never sexual in content, the gestures and the looks we gave one another suggested otherwise. We physically wanted each other, but because of our workplace environment, there was no way we could let on to our feelings. We could never sneak a kiss or a long sensual hug because in every hallway, in every corner, there were cameras always watching and we definitely were not going to jeopardize our livelihoods. Looking back on it now, I thank God for the security cameras because if they were not there it could have possibly been some inappropriate touching going on between us. A touch here, a touch there, and maybe a kiss somewhere. Thank you, God for the restrictions you placed around us.

After a while I found myself uncontrollably thinking about another woman's husband on a regular basis. I couldn't seem to shake the thought of him. The more he entered my thought pattern, the more I yearned for him physically. While all this was transpiring in my mind, I was still portraying to be a happy mother, wife and woman in ministry because I truly thought I was. To be completely honest, at that moment in my life, it felt like I was the happiest I'd been in a long time. We sent a few text messages to each other, spoke on the phone several times; just basically wanting to hear each other's voice. I couldn't wait for Monday – Fridays because that meant I got to see him. Boy did I hate the weekends. I got so wrapped up in this man emotionally till it was unreal and had not laid a finger sexually on him. How could you desire someone so bad without experiencing sex with them? Only God knows what kind of emotional state I would have been in if we would have had sexual intercourse. Yes, I loved my husband, my marriage, my life, but I wanted this man badly. I knew in my heart this relationship could never be. Just look at what happened to me almost a decade ago. Why was I not thinking about what I went through and the end result? My husband came home to me, HIS WIFE. Why didn't I think this man would do the same thing? Yet still I wanted what I wanted. The way he looked at me, how he complemented me on things I'd never been complemented on, how he yielded his attention to me, even down to how he questioned things about me turned me on and I wanted more of it. There were times I thought of me and this man possibly being a couple for real. But reality was not far behind in my thoughts. What was I going to do with my husband and children if I pursued this married man? My reputation would be ruined for good. I am a mother of 4 children, how childish and irresponsible of me to be in this place. All these questions mattered to me, but what also mattered were these feelings I was experiencing for the first time for another man in my 14 year marriage. At times I thought I was going crazy, but my flesh craved him and I couldn't control it. By now my lust for him was on fleek. What would happen if we were ever alone? Would I actually go all the way?

There were times I truly wanted to if the opportunity presented itself. No other man had touched me in the 14 years of my marriage and I took pride in that, but was I willing to throw it all away? Was I going to become a statistic? You know the saying of cheaters, "Everyone cheats", which is a familiar and common statement concerning people who have been cheated on or a person who cheats repeatedly. It was a struggle not to act upon my everyday impulses. Seeing him every day made me happy and also made things more difficult. I anticipated seeing him walk in my office throughout the day. At times I felt like such a hypocrite because here I am a married woman, yet still I had a strong lust monkey on my back that would not lose its grip. I lived in constant fear of what could happen between us and who could find out. Where was the Godly ways, principles, values I'd learned and held on to so tightly before? There were times I did not want this in my life and other times I enjoyed it. Coming home to my husband and trying to interact with him was often difficult. I am pretty sure he could feel my attention span run out on him. It wasn't his fault, it was mine. I brought the thoughts of this man into my home. When I should have had my husband on my mind I had him on my mind. When I should have been communicating with my husband, I was emotionally connecting more to this man. My flesh and the spirit of lust had a special bond and I was caught in the middle. I loved my boss at the time and we had an awesome relationship, but when it was time to come out of what I was in, God caused her and my relationship to go sour, which forced me to resign. It is my firm belief concerning our testing season, there is a start date and an end date. The end date can be altered depending on the one being tested. If you follow Gods instructions, the test will end at its appointed time. But if you follow your flesh, you can prolong the test. The fact that my boss totally started treating me like crap made me seek employment elsewhere because our relationship had gotten just that bad. I was so angry at her and didn't realize God was using this scenario to present the escape door. If everything had stayed great between her and my relationship, I would have stayed at that job in those surroundings. God knows what it will take to initiate a vacate notice to a season in our lives. The relationship between he and I never made it past the work place and once I resigned from that job, I thought I was rescued and the whole ordeal was over, but that was so far from the truth.

Even after I could no longer see him physically, emotionally I did all the time. I would think about him and wonder if he was thinking about me. After that became a routine in my thought pattern, I then realized the real danger I was in. The thoughts of him enslaved my mind and spoke to every part of my being. The flirting did not last long but the desire to flirt did. It took a long time for those desires to stop. It wasn't until my husband found out about the situation that the 1 ½ year bondage of carrying the burden of what happened broke off my mind completely. It's true what they say, "A mind is a terrible thing to waste", which is so easy to do if you let it entertain things it shouldn't. I've learned with our mind we can create a false reality when our thoughts are allowed to entertain illusions.

The day was going great at work and I wasn't expecting this type of text from my husband. All of a sudden, a text message flashed across my phone screen. Me of course, I'm expecting a little love saying, a cute picture of him or maybe a little sexting perhaps, but that never happened.

IT CAN HAPPEN — DARRYL & MONICA

I will never forget the gut wrenching questions & pictures my husband sent me on the day he found out about the affair. As soon as I opened the message, the other guy's face, one I thought I would never see again, popped up. In that second, I literally felt my heart sink into my stomach. It felt like being on a roller coaster at the climax of the ride and all of a sudden plunging head first into the deepest, darkest tunnel. After opening his text, there I was at my desk speechless and terrified. I didn't know how to reply or even know if I should. Immediately, questions like how he got these pictures and how did he find out raced back and forth in my mind. I thought he would never come into the knowledge of what happened. I often hoped Darryl wouldn't find out or anyone else. Then I thought of how he may have. Within that moment, the other guy's wife came to mind. She had already sent words of expressions to me once she found out, so I figured she contacted my husband. Before Darryl found out, a big part of me felt like he shouldn't know because it was no big deal, since I had never slept with this guy. So to me, there was no harm done. Then there were times I kind of wished he knew because I hated carrying the secret and thinking one day it would be revealed.

I would often revert back to the thoughts of I only had a few inappropriate exchanged words with him, no biggie. When I was confronted, it was like an atomic bomb exploded in my heart. When the affair was exposed, it was like shinning a bright LED light in a dungeon. All the filth of the affair was illuminated and for the first time I could see it for what it really was. As long as it was a secret and no one knew about it, the real truth of my actions was hidden, but when it was exposed, it was like scales fell from my eyes and I saw the raw ugliness of it all. I then fully understood that I had committed adultery against my husband and that I was wrong. The moment I grabbed the knob of that slightly opened door, I became an adulterer. **Proverbs 23:7**, *"So a man thinketh in his heart, so is he."* I was equally as wrong as my husband when he had his sexual affair. Thoughts of me possibly losing my marriage began to replay. So, I did what any wrong, caught in their mess spouse would do. I tried to act like it was nothing and downplay the incident, which basically means I tried to lie. He asked, "Who is this?" I replied, "Oh he used to be a co-worker." More questions began to follow. "What happened between you and him?" By this time my heart is racing, my palms are sweating and I'm just wishing this moment never happened. Not only that, but I'm scared and trying to play it cool, all while being at work. I remember all I wanted to do was get to him, so we could talk face to face. So finally, I broke down and told him what happened. He was furious yet calm, which scared me because I didn't know how to gage the level of his feelings. Later that night, we met for dinner to further discuss the situation in private. Still calmer than I thought he should be, we talked sensibly about the situation although, it was extremely uncomfortable for me more than I let on. He only wanted to know small details, unlike me when I wanted to know the ins and outs of his affair and I asked it all. Was he going to forgive me? Even if he did, was I going to be able to forgive myself? Shame and guilt was tearing me up by this point. I couldn't believe that the woman he thought I was had been exposed for having this type of flaw.

As I sat there looking at him I realized how much I loved him and how wrong I was for putting us in this predicament. I looked at him with such conviction and I assured him that night at the restaurant table, that I wanted our marriage. I sincerely apologized and asked him for forgiveness. He looked at me and he forgave me. Truthfully, I left that restaurant feeling afraid for my marriage. From that moment we went on again, rebuilding our love, our trust in one another and our commitment to this special love bond that we share. Not once did he ever bring it back up or use it to throw stones. It was like it never happened. He actually took the blame for it and stated that he had let this spirit in our home years ago. What a mature thing to say, but I did not accept him taking the blame for my actions. After all, I knew better. Although I thank God for the level of humility my husband displayed concerning my downfall, at the same time, the mere thought of him now knowing of my behavior made me sink to a low place within myself. See I had always thought concerning marital affairs, that there was no way Monica could ever get caught up like that. It was absolutely impossible for me to ever stoop that low and personally, my thoughts towards people who did were nasty and the scum of the earth. I'd seen so much devastation and so many marriages torn apart behind it and I was too right with God to be named among them folk who participated in such a sin. The one who thinks he/she is above certain temptations could be setting themselves up for a haughty fall experience. As I sat with him, I wondered was he really going to be able to trust me again. Could the knowledge of my prior actions possibly drive him to do what he had done before? Was this going to be a back and forth every ten years occurrence in our marriage? I chose to block all negative thoughts and focused on us having a healthy marriage.

My Godly wisdom to women all over the world is never think you are above temptation because you're not. Temptation has no preference. That spirit tries all sizes, nationalities, genders and ages. As women, don't ever look at another woman and compare her shortcomings to yours. We say all the time what we will never do, and we say it loosely. We don't know what tomorrow holds. If and when temptation presents itself to you, no matter what it is, it does not mean you did something wrong or you provoked it. Temptation is what it is. This spirit will use anything or anybody and often presents itself at an unexpected time to try to entice you and entangle you. It can in the beginning seem small and harmless, but temptation NEVER intends to stay the same size it was when it first presented itself. It will seize every opportunity to GROW and EXPAND in your life. Temptation wants you to give it life for the sole purpose of taking over your life. So much to the point it could literally end your life. The entire time I was emotionally entangled, there were times I called on God to help me, crying for Him to rescue me, but it seemed like the more I wanted help, the more it wouldn't come. So I found myself right back glued to the idea of being with this man. Looking back on that experience in my life, I now know I was dealing with a force that was greater than my own strength and will. It literally had me in a headlock and refused to let me go. I knew I loved my husband and ultimately wanted my family. I knew I didn't want to experience guilt and shame behind a terrible scandal. I did not want the titles of being a hoe, home-wreaker, slut, adulterer and everything else they call you when you tango outside of your marriage.

I can truly say it was nobody but Gods power that encamped around me during this trying time in my life. His grace, mercy, forgiveness and love was there with me while I was falling into a pit and that same grace, mercy, forgiveness and love lifted me out of that pit. It felt like I was literally being swallowed up by this stronghold, but God made a way of escape for me right on time. He took me physically out of my surroundings so that I wouldn't have to face that temptation every day. That's a true saying, out of sight out of mind in many instances, but the process of being delivered is not complete. For me, after some time, the less I saw him with my natural eyes, made me forget about him more and more. If a person can somehow remove themselves from the physical place temptation has set up camp, that one act alone can at least help initiate the deliverance process. There will be times you've removed yourself physically, but the soul tie will still be in tact so to the point you feel like you are still in that environment. Then the flip side of it is you can remove yourself physically from that environment and the soul tie can become aggressively stronger because now the distance has caused a deeper longing in your soul. Once I processed all those crazy but real emotions I was experiencing, that's when I knew it was more than just a physical location that held me connected. I discovered I was dealing with something that was deeper than I anticipated. This attraction was deeply rooted, and I needed deliverance for my soul and my mind. When you are caught up in lust *(fantasy illuminated)*, a soul tie causes blurred vision concerning what's most important to you. You are unable to fully understand what's all at stake. You do not clearly see the possible consequences of your actions. It's like living in a diluted reality where nothing is clear. Lastly, lust cripples you to the point you don't realize there is a strong dysfunction and that you seriously need help. I desperately needed the aide of the Holy Spirit and I needed someone in the physical as well that I could talk to. But I lived in constant fear of someone judging me. I felt I had no one I could talk to and I felt alone, dealing with this new devil all by myself. How could the one who prayed for people, who gave counsel to others, who was a beacon of light for some, be the one who is in need of someone concerning something like this? I didn't want anybody to know I had fallen prey to lust and was entangled by a soul tie. What would people think of me now?

Let me share with you three things that allowed my deliverance to be complete:

> 1. It was the removal from him and an environment that was conducive to my desires.
>
> 2. It was the desire to be free; the deliverance I asked God for in my prayers.
>
> 3. It was the exposing of the truth to my husband.

Let me just piggy back on #3 because this is what I failed to do, which kept me in bondage longer. If you are married and you have experienced a soul tie with another individual outside your spouse and you never tell your spouse, you are not FREE. How can you be when you are harboring this secret? And because this is a secret means you have not asked your spouse for forgiveness for committing adultery. Even if it was not sexual in nature, you still gave what belonged to your spouse to another. Body, heart, mind, soul and everything in between, belong to your spouse only.

You are getting up going to work, working out, taking the kids to school and living your everyday life with unconfessed sins & offenses against your spouse. You have violated your covenant and it needs to be addressed. You cannot heal what has not been revealed. This is extremely important.

I don't know all the reasons why I was allowed to go through this trial, but I do know our testimonies are meant to help strengthen someone else. One of the lessons the Father wanted to teach me was how it's possible for good, God loving people like my husband, myself, and others to fall prey to things we never imagined. Now let me say this, if this is your lifestyle, then I am not speaking on your behalf. This message is for people who have fallen in a rut, not people who stay in a rut. This is not intended for repeated offenders who never come into their freedom. When the offense is done against us, it's something how we call the offender ungodly names and think the worse of them like I did when others fell into temptation. But when I fell, I didn't want to be thought of in any degrading manner because it was truly just a mistake when I committed the sin. I was able to see that those who had fallen were not people who deserved death, a stiff jail sentence or some other unbearable punishment. When I was betrayed I wanted the Lord to strike the side chick down right where she stood. On the other hand, I ultimately wanted nothing but good for my husband, although he really hurt me to the core. Yes, the act is horrible and renders excruciating pain, especially if it's done to you or someone you love. But oh, what grace and mercy we want if we fall and afflict that same hurt on other people. God has a way of teaching us compassion for those we refuse to have compassion for. That person who commits the sin is still loveable and well deserving of forgiveness too. There are great deals of people who do not intentionally set out to commit adultery or any other sin. When we as human beings get weak, selfish, hard headed, let our guard down, let people in our lives who we shouldn't and when we are ignorant of the devil's devices, things can happen. People we must love, we must forgive, we must move forward, no matter what we encounter. To all those who have entertained anything I've talked about in this book, even if you caused the hurt, just know that we serve a loving & forgiving God. All He asks from us is to repent of our sins, accept Him into our hearts and move forward. Know that I love you and I am praying for you, for I know all too well how it feels to be the offended and the offender...

His Story

For better or worse, richer or poorer was the constant phrase that seemed to constantly knock at my door. When you've seen, heard, watched, read and now you're the one involved... instead of running & hiding, stop! Wait! Why am I lying to myself, with myself, for myself?
Like 702 said, "Get It Together", because I might end up by myself!

THE FIGHT

What was it about those times I spent growing up and making memories with the Jackson family, while going over to Roger Street in between church service? It was special moments like practicing in the back room with our church youth rap team, or I know, that one particular time we shared that kiss on the church bus coming back from evening service. Yeah, that would be my last church bus trip of course. I remember IT happening for my good at a rehearsal one night. Wait, before I go to that particular night, let me address the fact that rejection can be a hurtful thing if it's not carefully addressed. I remember being in a place of seeking and really didn't know it. I had been turned down two times by ones that I felt met the description of Mrs. Sampson, well at least a girlfriend. I recall after the last let downs I found myself upstairs on King Street feeling hurt, down and unaware of the fact that I was sinking into a depression. I wasn't a beer drinker, but I found myself indulging in several beers to try to ease the pain. While I didn't find any ease, I did recognize a bible that was sitting on the shelf. It was one of those Gideon bibles that you would find in a Holiday Inn hotel. I know it wasn't mine. I believe we packed it by mistake from a recent Kappa Beach Party. I began to flip through it and Proverbs 18:22 said, *"A man that findeth a wife..."* those words stuck out and really grabbed my attention. It was as if God was speaking directly to me and my current situation. It wouldn't be long before that scripture took precedence in my life. So about that rehearsal night at church, it wasn't anything different than a normal bible study and choir rehearsal, so I thought. It was towards the end of bible study and for some odd reason most of the youth *(young men/teens)* happened to be sitting in the rear pews of the church. I noticed Monica Jackson in a way I'd never noticed her before and the way the homies heads were turning, so did they. You would think she walked past us on purpose the way everything panned out, but in actuality, all she wanted was a chance to get up and go to the restroom in peace. If staring was against the law that entire back row of teens would have had a huge fine to pay. I remember it like yesterday. That blue denim skirt she was wearing, oh and that sexy character silky material blouse. I was paying so much attention to the details, I didn't realize I had finally laid eyes on who was going to become my promise.

It's kind of crazy how out of all the years of being around her, for some reason, this particular night of seeing her was different than the others. Not only did she catch my attention, she also captured my heart, so to the point I literally felt myself gasp for a deep breath. I'm not just writing these words to sound deep to those reading, my heart literally adjusted to another rhythm of love that particular night. That night ideally became history for the both of us. Well let's just say I had my first experience with the prophetic. Never had I approached a female that I was interested in with such authority and poise. You know that God had to have been in it because of my bold pursuit. I went to her before she entered the choir loft and told her straight up, "Monica, girl if you weren't taken I would put a ring on your finger." Now you would have thought my palms would have been sweaty, but man look, I was so confident in what I was doing. She responded back by saying, "I'm not taken." By this time I was high fiving myself. I grabbed a piece of paper and made sure I took the correct digits down. Let's just say rehearsal for me that night was very special. You would get a sense that everything from this point would grow in harmony just as everything else had, but not so. We had to establish our courtship on the low because of how others would view it. Not trying to honk my own horn, but there was one particular female who was crushing on me so to the point of pushing me into her *(Monica's)* arms. Yeah, a "friends, how many others have them" type of situation. Not only was I honestly digging Monica, but I wanted to be with Monica. After I disclosed to her how I felt, she turned me down because of her loyalty to her friend crushing on me. I will say Monica is a great person to have as a friend. She will hold you down till the end. I had to go to her mama for wisdom to get her to accept the fact that it was ok to open up to me and take what we felt to the next level. It would be that conversation which led us to, or should I say lead her to becoming the woman of my dreams. Once we decided to go public with our relationship, it seemed as if all hell broke loose. I had lots of friends and others I really looked up to looking down on the very idea of Monica and Darryl becoming a couple. I had so many grand slam dinner meetings at I-Hop and phone conversations concerning what other people had to say and thoughts concerning us. At the time I was living with my cousin and it was constantly the three of us in one room, but we made it work. My cousin's phone would ring with one's opinions as to how he needed to encourage me not to date her.

It was so to the point it seemed like we were picked out to be picked on by many at our place of worship at the time. From the hearsay and extra chats in the parking lots and trust me, it was way more negative stuff going on within the local congregation than our desires of being together. Our simply wanting to be together had gained the attention neither one of us was expecting. My parents weren't too happy about my decision, especially once I made the choice to move in with her and her mom. I had my own room that belonged to my deceased brother-in-law, Michael. This came about after long talks and prayer about us becoming one. Yes, we married fast. We had this theory we wanted to make it right. After all, our parents did raise us right. I'm 19 and she was 21 and we had a 3 month old baby. She was 3 years older and had been an adult a little longer than I had. She had her own car and I was a scrub, you know the passenger hanging out the side of my cousins' ride… you remember that song. She would take me to my job at the airport, pick me up and even at times let me keep her car to go to drumming engagements from time to time. So I could understand my parents reserve a little, but it wasn't enough to get me to give up on what we were trying to establish. Hell yeah, we were hot to trot, but there was also that fear of we must stop and wait until we are united as one. So yes, the closer we came to getting married, I moved in and that only added gasoline to the flames that were already burning. One thing that hurt me most was when I was asked to give up playing the drums at church and Monica was asked to step down from the choir.

Don't get me wrong, I understand the stance, but seeing others being able to continue in their dirt hurt like hell and there was proof that you could find on them right under the nails of their fingers. Needless to say, we were obedient. We sat down and a few months later she would be walking down the aisle looking beautiful as she could be. The week before our wedding and all that had taken place leading up to it suddenly didn't matter anymore. Seemed like nothing else could go wrong, but I ended up losing my temp job assignment. So now we are limited in funds to a certain degree. I was still a firm believer that when it's meant to be it's going to be regardless. Some would have said, well maybe this is your sign that's it's not meant Darryl, but that thought never crossed my mind. God sent what we needed exactly when we needed it. I gave our wedding coordinator $100.00 and everything else was paid for. From decorations, wedding dress, reception and even the hotel room for the night. June 19, 1999, we started dating and August 21, 1999 was my prophecy to Monica coming to pass, not even a year later. It had to have been God ordained because everything felt so right. We would go on to love the way God intended for us to, not really focusing on the challenges that were waiting down the road for us on our journey. All we had was our son and each other to love on. I was living on top of a pinnacle! I loved me some Monica. Our beginning was full of hard hits and late night cries, but we always would fall back on what our parents taught us to do and that was to pray. It's what kept us strong and safe during the fight. I never imagined that 1999 would be filled with so much life altering, life changing events. We would go on and live out the next phase of our lives together. I always knew that I had a praying woman because her mom was a praying woman. I too watched my Dad lead prayer during devotion on Sunday mornings, so we had a relationship with God and were well adverse in scripture. We knew how to go to God by way of prayer. This is how we began building our unit, obtaining jobs, a car and our own place to live, which were our goals.

THE GREAT WAKEUP

A close friend/brother gave me a lot of encouraging words and wisdom during our first year of being together. He said if we could make aim towards seven years we would be ok. Little did he know I took his words to heart. So I went from just focusing on the now, to actually building for the future; which is not spoken of now a days. No, there's not a step-by-step manual on how to have a successful marriage, but if others like us, are willing to be transparent and share their marital journey, that alone would help so many use wisdom prior to saying, "I do".

We need to encourage couples that hardships are to be expected but, it all goes into building your marital house. Each brick has a placement, each placement determines a room, space or area and they all require a process before and definitely after it's properly built. By now, we've grown/matured a little more, as husband and wife. There were things I was ignorant to, like not apologizing when I was wrong. Monica and I would finish each other's sentences and be on one accord in thought often. Everything so far was good. Then there arose an issue I was not too familiar with. We went from good loving to absolutely nothing. I didn't understand what was soon to happen in our union as a result of this issue. I ignored it and just like every other thing, I prayed about it and gave it to God. It was around this time God was really pulling and tugging on me. I was thirsty for Him even while this unexpected, unfamiliar visitor showed its head, but once again, I didn't yield any attention to addressing it. I would go on to accept my call into ministry, all while this visitor was permanently present. To our union three girls, Me'Lady *(2001)* and several years later the twins Sierra & Kierra *(2004)* were born so our family extended tremendously. Good jobs, a house, both of us in ministry, a beautiful family and still this unexpected visitor had become a part of our household unit. As the head of my house I allowed it to remain by not addressing it through the years. It became bold and would stand in the way of God ordained worship between a husband and wife from time to time. It was not an all the time occurrence obviously because we had children.

It kept quiet until it eventually gained enough power to cause damage. There were times my promise was not in the mood and it became more of not being in the mood than usual. At times it was if I was pressuring her, so I would just go without. Once again, being young and grey, I still had a level of patience that's only given by God. She'd just given birth to our beautiful twins and the pregnancy alone took a major toll on her. I was right there with her the entire time, so I could sympathize with her. I had just received a promotion at a major A/C corporation, so life was good on that end.

One day I received a letter in the mail addressed to me at home saying, "Hi Darryl, it's been awhile. Hadn't heard or seen you. I will be in your city soon and hope to catch up with you." Talk about being spooked, because there was no return address, and neither was there a signature stating who this mysterious letter was from. Not to mention if you were not family or a church member, I had no dealings with you. I didn't really pay it any attention until I received the letter again at work. When I received the one at home I did tell Monica. God is so wise in His ways and we must learn to follow His wisdom through to the very end. I recall sitting down and explaining the letter to Monica and asking her to keep me before the Lord in the next upcoming season like never before. To be honest I had no clue as to why I was even having this conversation with her, especially to this magnitude. I was sensitive to God and believed He was sending me warnings of what was to come soon. It wouldn't be long before I would be asking myself how did I get in this situation? Ya'll, I messed up bad and was enjoying the mistake & mishap of cheating on the one I pegged the name Promise in the above paragraphs. I thought I was enjoying where I was at that time, but somewhere in my heart and mind I knew it was wrong and there were opportunities to stop, but I ignored them all. It only takes one tangle to get caught up and then comes the possibility of tripping, and boy I was tripped up something bad.

God eventually showed himself mighty in this matter, although the situation became ugly for a while. One incident I remember the VP of manufacturing embracing me in the rainy parking lot after discovering that my vehicle had been vandalized on company property. The damages that occurred were slashed tires *(all four)*, shattered rear & front window, a keyed hood & doors, busted head lights, etc. Let's just say my car looked like it barely survived a round of street fighter *(for those of us that can remember)*. All of this was a result of Monica finding out about me cheating. The VP of manufacturing followed me to the nearest discount tire and purchased me four brand new tires. He left me there as I waited for them to finish with my car. Immediately I started to reflect on the hurt I was causing everyone, especially the directly involved spouses. They didn't deserve the hurt and the pain. Mind you, I was the man of God in this.

Not only did it need to stop, but it needed to stop NOW. After a few days I would be back at home with my family starting the healing process. You would think that at this point this would be easy, but it really was the most humiliating and embarrassing moments of my entire life. The get back up again song by Pastor Donnie McClurkin was easier sung and so uncomfortable, but it was a part of the process. Almost like having to study but still not ready to retest. See, all that I had experienced at that point placed me in a position of humbling myself again because I stepped out of that realm of holiness and had to go through it all over again. I thought I had it together after taking a stand, when all parties were against us in the beginning. Now, I found myself nearly five years later in a stumbled state.

One statement that continually played in my mind was what my friend Tim Jones encouraged me with. He said, "If you can make it to 7 years you will be ok." Now, I was faced with the prospect of us not making it through the next few hours or days. I had caused so much damage, hurt, disrespect and shame. As a minister of the gospel, this was an unusual position to be in as all of my personal business was aired out at my local church. Just to think about the fight we had to endure in the beginning of our relationship; when we announced our relationship, as a couple, to the church. Now, the church had a reason to hate me; this was a lot to handle. While dealing with all of this, I received a glimpse of hope. While Monica had every reason to move on with her life, she still wanted me. I asked myself, "*Why would she want to stay with me?*" Let's face it, she didn't do anything wrong. Ok, so there was a lack of affection from time to time, but she still didn't deserve the right to be hurt like I hurt her.

Once I realized that I hurt her, I was willing to face any consequences associated with my wrong doing, even if it meant losing my family. God knows that would have killed me. Not having any access to Monica is one thing, but my children is another. Not being able to kiss, hold, touch and see them when I wanted to, lying down at night knowing my heartbeats are ok on the other side of the wall would have literally killed me. Not being able to see Monica's smile and her being there to push me as she always did would literally have sent me to an early grave. As sad as this may sound outside of my immediate family, there was no life. They were and are still my life today. So that glimpse of hope I had when she expressed how she wanted to make things work blessed me, but at the same time, I really didn't know how to feel. I tempted to think she was going to get me home and torture me for the pain I caused her and our family, although deep down inside I knew better than that. If anything, she wanted to "make-up" so that we could advance forward in life together. By the way, there is a blessing in the making up. I'm back home without a job, now no car and now this large "I'm a Cheater" sticker stamped on my chest (you will get that later after attending one of our empowerment sessions). Home was fine. Monica made my environment safe and healthy for the both of us. We talked about my infidelity and laughed at certain things like her going ballistic on my car. It was not until I would go outside my door that certain people would make me feel like I'd murdered or even had a disease by way of their actions towards me. It was so bad at times. They didn't even have to say a word, it was just their actions alone. We must be extra careful how we handle people; what we assume to know about them and their stormy situations. I remember so clear wanting to drive my car right off of the beltway and 290 interchange highway because of other's assumptions. Not only did I have people who I thought to be close stoning me because of my actions, I myself wanted to stone me. Have you ever been in a large area crowded with people and felt like you were the scum at the bottom of their shoes and everyone in that crowd recognized you as just that? Even to the point of making sure others avoided you? That scenario played out just as hard in the church as it would at I-Hop diners. I just could not find peace in others. Was it wrong that everyone didn't welcome me back in love like others did? Was I wrong for feeling the way I felt? I eventually answered my own questions. Many times in life we all will screw up and mess up.

Sometimes worse than others, but it's our place as that individual to get up from whatever circus or parade people try to make us a part of. I was so baffled by this because once the smoke cleared it was me, myself and I only in the show. I was upset and again embarrassed at Darryl. Darryl was trying to blame others for the pain caused by Darryl. I would wonder where are those ones who I could spill my heart out to and wouldn't be judged for the way I was feeling inside? I could have taken a number of invites I received on advising me not to marry her but where are you now that I was the one who messed up? I would eventually get over Darryl, so I thought. I was really freed up from the opinion of men and how they felt, but I still hadn't faced Darryl. My guilty conscience weighed heavy on me and I found myself living a hopeless fictional reality. I was careful handling Monica at that time. I didn't want her to know that I was battling with the fear of thinking that she would possibly entertain the thought of wanting to get back at me. I always said that if that was the case I'd rather not know. If I can be honest, I feared her past showing back up in her life and reclaiming what people felt I didn't deserve or giving her what I couldn't offer, especially after what I did. This thought stems from her family/friends and the possibility of that happening played in my head every day. I was suffocating subconsciously and didn't even realize it. I knew that I needed help but I was afraid and embarrassed to reach out and ask. Also, it's difficult to ask when people around you make you out to be dirt. If I may say, it's ok to ask for wisdom or help when and while struggling with issues. An old wise one once said to me, "Closed mouths don't get fed." I admonish you to reach out to someone you can trust to pour out your heart to for the sake of healing.

This was a dangerous time for us both, simply because I didn't want to push her in someone else's direction. The battle in my mind was a serious situation and if attention was not brought to it things could have turned out completely different. As this book digs deeper after my fall, there was a cross up email situation with Monica and someone from her past and I just so happen to be cc'd on it. It was nothing bad in content just a conversation that shouldn't have gone forth with this particular individual. I even made the mistake of conversing via text with someone and Monica found it. Nothing bad again, but it's these tech savvy devices and systems that at times can keep the married community in trouble. One thing I've learned is man-made, men-chanical invention can spark negativity that eventually will expose itself. All of this and Darryl is still ignoring the man in the mirror. This led me to establishing hidden trust issues with Monica, so to the point of me asking her about her social media accounts. I even questioned in my mind if certain family members who knew about my prior infidelity would send messages to Monica from people she had a prior relationship with. These feelings would lie dormant in me until what I feared became reality.

EMOTIONAL ENTANGLEMENT

Now we're serving in many different capacities in ministry and our home life was good again. There we were seeing life in a different perspective. Our son is a basketball player with a few years left till graduation and the girls are busy singing, modeling and involved with theatre arts. One day I'm at work in an unbothered zone when a blocked message from Facebook appeared out of nowhere. It was someone else's wife reaching out to me with a message concerning the thing I feared the most. As crazy as this may sound, this was for me. I found myself having a breakdown in the mirror at work. What I was faced with was not the issue as a whole. I hadn't let go and hadn't trusted my own self. Not to mention the guilt of causing this upon myself. Shocked yes, surprised yes, hurt no. I was hurt more by not forgiving MYSELF for what I had done years ago. God gave me such a peace overall and even when I did want to get upset I couldn't come to grips to do so.

I actually found myself longing for a much more in-depth connection with that girl who caught my attention with that blue jean skirt at bible study trying to go to the restroom. I honestly think this happened because at the time I should have been focused on getting more in-depth with her, but instead I wasn't truly connected with the depth of my own identity. Yes, I missed out and suffered because of it. While on the phone with the wife from Facebook, I encouraged her and her husband both. I went home to my wife and had a heated discussion concerning the situation. I told her that I was not going anywhere and neither was she. I knew then that my heart had healed and what I had been holding on to was now broken off of me. So now we could move forward together without any disruptions. To this day I can honestly say that I vaguely remember all that occurred with that issue, which is why this dissertation is so short. I fell in love again with my promise (*name I'd given her back in 2005*). I had to come to a place of understanding that she was my everything and while I was busy draining our marriage by beating myself up, I was forfeiting and missing many opportunities to reconnect with her on a greater level. Would this have canceled out what just happened? I don't know, but it would have allowed us to be further along in our courtship relationship. This book perhaps would have been written three years prior. Staying at home this time had more weight and significance. We had our children to factor in as well. Not just for our children, but I loved Monica and I knew that God brought us together. Going through that season of packing up and leaving was old news, 18 years into our marriage, we should be well past going to mama's house to escape. Choosing to stay at home and working through things together only strengthens the marriage. Leaving only gives sand like strength to your union. You can become solid again when you're able to stand therein. So I stayed home and took a time out. Afterwards, I found myself falling deeper than deep in love with the woman I vowed to spend all the days of my life with.

The couples that are meant to be are those that go through everything designed to tear them apart and come out stronger.

IT CAN HAPPEN DARRYL & MONICA

IT CAN HAPPEN (Monica)

Marriage: *Two people coming together, walking this thing out called Life as one determined to be the happiest they can be no matter what.*

I often hear people say, concerning adultery, that this act is something they could not forgive, endure or put up with. If infidelity happens to take place in your marriage, I do believe there is still hope that the marriage could not only survive but thrive again.

When we truly love someone and want to make things work, we will change whatever we need to in order to make it right again. It all starts with a decision; with a choice. In today's society we are quicker to dismiss meaningful long term relationships when short term adversity threatens its existence. It is extremely important for couples to know when God's sign of redeeming power is in the midst, which are always demonstrated by actions. If the one who has been the offender truly changes their ways, then you know restoration is your portion. A true change is seen, felt and implemented on every level. Changing their buddies, the places they go, their phone number, etc. to totally distance themselves from those negative environments and behaviors, they are willing to do so and immediately.

Is the offender willing to give up all the foolishness and nonsense to save what is shared in the relationship? If that person is not, then you know where you two stand. Married couples, there is an again moment that can happen in your union.

Hosea in the bible literally paid a price to get his wife Gomer back. My question is if God said to you go and get your spouse back, what price are you willing to pay? Are you willing to pay with humility, patience, forgiveness and obedience? Would the cares of your best friend, your family, co-workers or even your own will overrule what God said? The thing I love about Hosea is even though his wife disrespected him on many levels, he did not seek revenge and he didn't hold it against her, but he chose to love her beyond his pain, in spite of his embarrassment and regardless of other's opinions and other options. People knew what his wife's extracurricular activities were, it was no secret. He reclaimed who God had given him and was willing to be called a fool for the sake of covenant.

My 19 years of being married to Mr. Darryl L. Sampson has rendered some of the most amazing and trying times of my life. There were victories I never thought we would obtain and there were heartaches I never thought we would endure. I've learned not to say what we will or won't go through. A lot of bad experiences will happen in a great marriage. Please know just because you are with the one God created for you does not guarantee you a stress less, problem free and drama exempt union. Seems like you may experience more trials when you have the one. It's just the enemy's way of trying to devour destiny that supersedes what we are feeling at those moments in the natural. The truth is, the two of you are divinely connected beings. Satan tempted Eve and she tempted Adam, who by no means were two ordinary people who decided to hook up. No, they were connected beyond what was visibly seen. She was from him and made for him. The enemy hates divine connections because divine relationships tend to leave a divine legacy.

I never imagined we would have 4 children, share such a bond that is so beautiful and a love that is a true reflection of God's love. I always wanted a fairytale love as many little girls do, but in life as we mature we discover there is no such thing. To me when we are fortunate to find our true love, it is so much greater than a fairytale. The true joy comes in lessons learned, wisdom earned and priceless experiences that deliver a type of love (agape) that transcends time. There is no manual or step by step book that guarantees a successful marriage. Being married is always a work in progress. It is an ongoing learning and growing experience that is constantly trying to teach us, whether we want the lessons or not. I married the love of my life 19 years ago and yes, if I could, there are some things I would do different, but then that would somehow alter what I now know. No matter what, we have come to the conclusion that we are simply better together period.

You want to start living your best life, have that dream marriage and bomb career? It's all possible. But know that there will be some moments that will not be pleasant in your pursuit. Never in a million years did I think we would encounter adultery, lies & brokenness to get to a place in our lives/marriage where there is complete faithfulness, beautiful truth, unconditional love and joy. There was a time I thought we'd lost the dance in our marriage, but I've discovered guilty feet do have rhythm, they're just off beat. What we needed to do was find the beat of our love again, that would then moderate the rhythm of our relationship.

Never did I think IT COULD HAPPEN where we would encounter rejection from countless people who despised our union, but now are tremendously blessed by our determination and dedication. I never imagined IT COULD HAPPEN 19 years later being in love with the same man, even though we experienced harsh trials that most couples don't recover from.

If we stay busy and focused on our goals, the positive IT CAN HAPPEN factor WILL HAPPEN. Meaning what we are expecting to happen will somehow present itself. Why? Because everything we set out to do will in some way bring glory back to God and help someone else along the journey. We are not taking credit for anything, neither giving it to anyone. It's all GOD. My prayers are now God put strategic people in strategic places, so they can experience the IT CAN HAPPEN factor in every area of their lives. Whatever your IT CAN HAPPEN requests are just believe and keep moving towards it because IT ALREADY HAS HAPPENED.

Therefore I tell you, whatever you ask in prayer, believe that you have received it, and it will be yours (**Mark 11:24,** *ESV*).

IT CAN HAPPEN (Darryl)

After so many years of living a life of continuous struggles, fights, infidelity incidents, trust issues and ignoring issues most would have not survived (in fact, many didn't survive), I stand here today to encourage all that IT CAN HAPPEN. There is the good and the bad factor within all marriages that comes along with the territory. What makes the difference is whether or not both sides decide to work through it all. Note, I said both have to decide. There must be a unified effort with both parties and if it is only one sided you will find your marriage in trouble again. Talking and communicating it out, I would have to say was therapy; it was for us at least. I sit back now and think about had not she first said, "Darryl, I want you back home to work things out", we wouldn't be able to share our reality with you today. Ecclesiastes 4:12 says, "Three are even better, for a triple-braided cord is not easily broken." Communication is a powerful tool that the enemy uses to defeat many relationships. The trap is set up by the devil to make you not feel like talking about it, which never resolves anything. It's during these times you must talk your ass off. Holding back only boils the situation, which eventually heats up enough to cause a burn. The perfect bowl of oatmeal or grits is meant to be stirred at some point. Well the stirring for your marriage is called communication. Not communicating, I like to say, is a part of deception. We must understand, since looks can be deceiving, there has to be a follow up after they get past the fact of hearing you say I'm fine. How is your conversation and who are you communicating with? How often are you communicating with him or her and most importantly, God? You are going to have to pray, it's a must.

What can you bring to the table in the form of conversation? Husbands, after you show and give her good loving, if she wants to talk about it and hadn't taken the lead, then I challenge you to start the conversation. I don't want to acknowledge statistics because our goal is to reverse stats. I will say if there was more communication in that particular area prior to my infidelity mess up, I would have saved our marriage the unnecessary strain. The signs are always there but it's our responsibility to say something. Don't give the devil any more room when it comes to paralyzing the communication component within our marriages. This is a big part of the work that goes into Holy Matrimony or like I say, union. I believe as couples we often forget that we became one and when there is a glitch (not just in communication, but all aspects), the union becomes somewhat weighted and crippled to the point of causing potential chaos and confusion. This is critical for us to pay attention to and when this happens and is ignored, we become renegades to our vows. I don't care if it was the traditional vows or from the heart. This was a factor in the both of us agreeing to remain in place regardless. All I think about was the "I promise to be true to you in good times and in bad, in sickness and in health". I was sick, she was sick, and our actions brought on this sickness in what I have declared as pivotal points in our union. During the vow part of our wedding ceremony, the Bishop asked me to repeat after him, *"I vow to love and honor you all the days of my life."* My heart is strengthened to this effect, because it was from the heart I learned the importance of following your heart in situations such as this.

YES, I could have moved on and so could Monica, but our hearts would not allow us to. Getting her out of my system would have been a disaster for my life. What we've come together to build and establish would have been difficult to forget when she's all I got and know. Waking up to someone else may have been good for the moment but was not healthy for a lifetime. The grass on the other side always has a different sprinkler system, just by chance they happen to be similar systems, you may want to check the timers. If we were not in place in the beginning, who are we to try and maintain another man's yard? Tend to your own yard/grass, though it may be burning brown and growing weeds. Try switching up your fertilization method. Examine how much time you are investing in watering your own home front. Surrounding yourself around strong noteworthy husbands is important; even a great marriage community is great. These serve as fertilization to the brown that signifies possible dead and damaged areas within your yard. Marriage counseling is beneficial before and during your union. People think that it's ok to just jump the broom without talking things out. It could work but believe me there is something there being ignored, unaddressed or even hidden. In all my years of marriage counseling and marrying others, counseling served its place and had its privileges. It's within this component you touch on the possibilities of IT CAN HAPPEN, the good and bad within what God ordained. The bible speaks clearly that a man that findeth a wife findeth a good thing. Understand your marriage is the vision, plan and even the will of God. So when we go contrary, we are going against the very plan and will of the Father. Those who desire or plan to marry, take the time out to not only fall deeply in love but get to know him or her. Check out what you're getting into beforehand. Learn what ticks each other off because I am pretty sure you already know what turns each other on. Learn your in-laws and give them the opportunity to get to know you. This is very important because at the end of the day it's supposed to be family over everything. Having that support system will go a long way. Lastly keep people out of your issues. If there is absolutely no one you can talk to, go to God. Bringing outsiders into your union can kill the plan and curse the union. If you factor what's all been said and keep God the head of your house, husband following pursuit, wife in place following, everything else has no choice but to come into alignment or get out the way. Trust me, IT CAN HAPPEN!

Hi, I'm Darryl and I APPROVE THIS MESSAGE. Signing off for now!

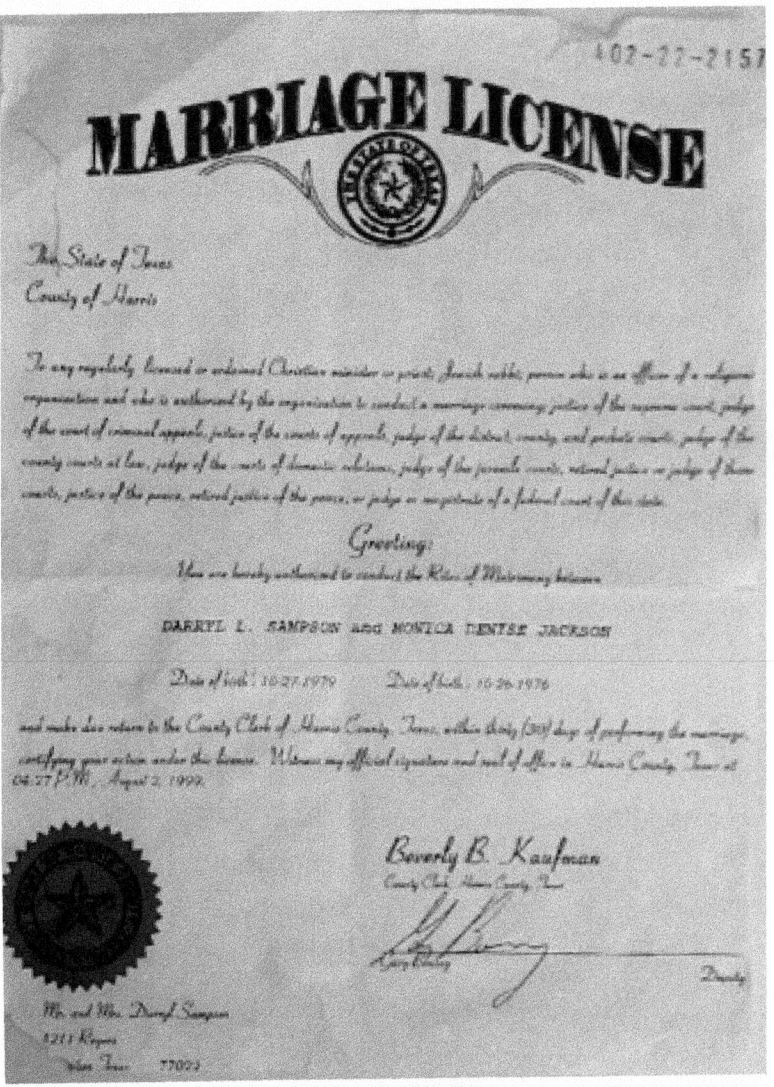

Thank you for supporting our story.
~Darryl & Monica

darrylmonica.com

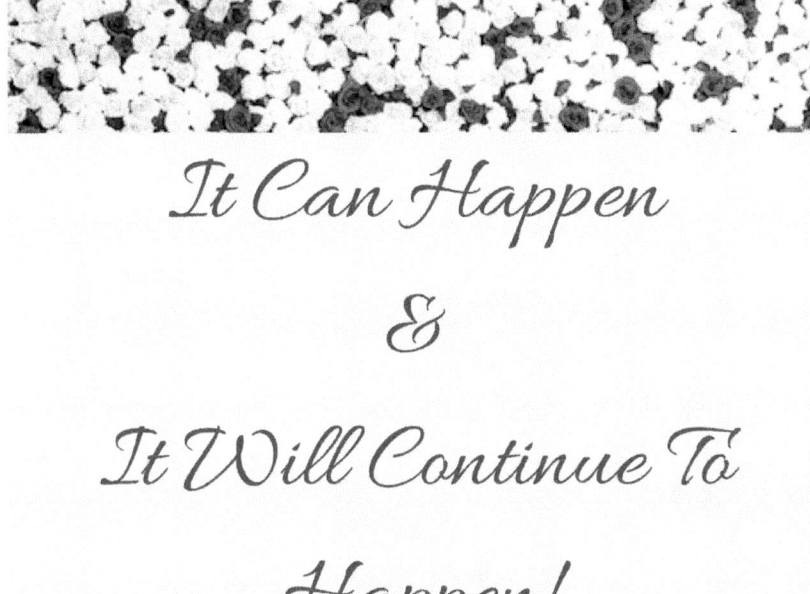

It Can Happen

&

It Will Continue To Happen!

To GOD Be The Glory.

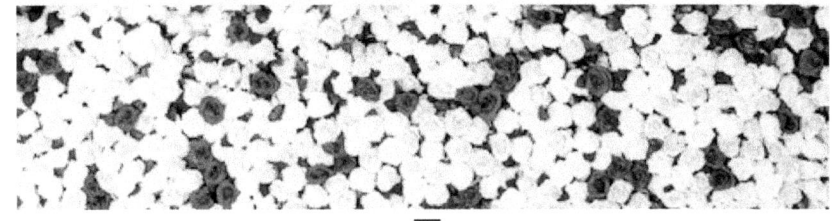

www.ingramcontent.com/pod-product-compliance
Lightning Source LLC
Chambersburg PA
CBHW051947160426
43198CB00013B/2343